T0195830

# Becoming a
# VICTOR!

*No Longer Just Surviving.*

VERONICA ROBERSON

WESTBOW
PRESS®
A DIVISION OF THOMAS NELSON
& ZONDERVAN

This book is a work of non-fiction. Unless otherwise noted, the author and the publisher make no explicit guarantees as to the accuracy of the information contained in this book and in some cases, names of people and places have been altered to protect their privacy.

WestBow Press books may be ordered through booksellers or by contacting:

WestBow Press
A Division of Thomas Nelson & Zondervan
1663 Liberty Drive
Bloomington, IN 47403
www.westbowpress.com
1 (866) 928-1240

Because of the dynamic nature of the Internet, any web addresses or links contained in this book may have changed since publication and may no longer be valid. The views expressed in this work are solely those of the author and do not necessarily reflect the views of the publisher, and the publisher hereby disclaims any responsibility for them.

Any people depicted in stock imagery provided by Getty Images are models, and such images are being used for illustrative purposes only.
Certain stock imagery © Getty Images.

Scripture quotations marked (NIV) are taken from the Holy Bible, New International Version®, NIV®. Copyright © 1973, 1978, 1984, 2011 by Biblica, Inc.™ Used by permission of Zondervan. All rights reserved worldwide. www.zondervan.com The "NIV" and "New International Version" are trademarks registered in the United States Patent and Trademark Office by Biblica, Inc.™

Scripture quotations marked (NLT) are taken from the Holy Bible, New Living Translation, copyright ©1996, 2004, 2015 by Tyndale House Foundation. Used by permission of Tyndale House Publishers, Inc., Carol Stream, Illinois 60188. All rights reserved.

Scripture quotations marked (KJV) taken from the King James Version of the Bible.

Scripture quotations marked (ESV) are from The ESV® Bible (The Holy Bible, English Standard Version®), copyright© 2001 by Crossway, a publishing ministry of Good News Publishers. Used by permission. All rights reserved.

Scripture taken from the New King James Version®. Copyright © 1982 by Thomas Nelson. Used by permission. All rights reserved.

ISBN: 978-1-9736-7265-4 (sc)
ISBN: 978-1-9736-7266-1 (e)

Library of Congress Control Number: 2019912042

Print information available on the last page.

WestBow Press rev. date: 08/19/2019

## 1 John 5:4, 5

For everyone born of God overcomes the world. This is the victory that has overcome the world, even our faith. [5] Who is it that overcomes the world? Only the one who believes that Jesus is the Son of God. (NIV)

# Becoming A VICTOR!

As a child, I attended a Baptist church. When my parents separated, I began attending service with my mother, who had become a Jehovah's Witness. For many years I searched for God and His Glory, but always felt as if I was unworthy of His love and mercy.

My life was full of pain and disappointment. I endured verbal abuse from a close family member. I was molested several times under the age of ten. Even though my mother took me to counseling, I never got over that experience. I was raped a few months before my sixteenth birthday. I endured judgement by people solely for being raised in a single-parent household. At the age of eighteen it was confirmed that I would never have children due to severe endometriosis. Every mistake I made seemed to be evaluated by others as the ultimate offense, regardless of the hay in their own eyes. By the time I went off to college, I was just moving through the motions of meeting expectations. When I was not studying, I was drinking the pain away.

At the age of twenty-five, I fully gave my life to Jesus. I was baptized and through marriage counseling, I was able to overcome years of hurt and disappointment.

I assure you this journey was not easy, but with God all things are possible. As you read each chapter, I pray you find the guidance you need to become a victor. Do not hesitate to see a therapist. Receiving counsel does not make you weak. I recommend seeking guidance as much as possible in the beginning and a check-up every five years. Even when you think you have overcome, one misfortune can send you spiraling down a rocky road. This does not mean you lack faith; it means you are weak and need God and counseling.

# Contents

Chapter 1    Forgiveness, For Real! ..................................................................1

Chapter 2    Man said, "No." God said, "Yes." ...................................................9

Chapter 3    Finding Purpose ........................................................................ 17

Chapter 4    Overcoming Untruths ................................................................ 23

Chapter 5    Victor vs. Survivor! .................................................................. 29

# Chapter One

# Forgiveness, For Real!

"Make allowance for each other's' faults, and forgive anyone who offends you."
– (Colossians 3:13, NLT)

Could my face look any more confused and upset?

What does she mean when she says she will no longer be prescribing medicine?

What is *holistic* medicine and what does it have to do with my medicine?

As I became more upset the doctor's words became mumbles. My fear of not making it home before my vision was impacted by the approaching migraine was the only thing I could think about. Before I knew it, I was yelling at my once favorite doctor.

"Look doctor. You and I both know what happens when migraines take over. Last week, during rush hour, I was forced to pull over and call the paramedics to bring me to the hospital. I could not see a thing due to the blinding pain!"

The doctor calmly replied, "I understand where you are coming from. At the same time, you need to identify the triggers for your migraines. Switching medicines every six months is not a lifestyle you have to live. The next time you feel a migraine approaching, write down what you were thinking about."

A migraine was approaching now, and she was the root cause!

As I gathered my belongings and exited the room she left me with a few more words.

"You have to deal with the hurt. Please take my advice and write down what you are thinking about, as soon as you feel the migraine approaching," the doctor said.

I wish I could say I applied her advice during my next migraine. I did not. I went to many more doctors. All the other doctors agreed with me, my favorite doctor was a quack. I continue to switch medicines. I tried different treatments, including shock therapy. Nothing stopped the migraines. The medicine would relieve the tension, allowing me to live somewhat a normal life.

Almost two years later, I was sitting on the couch holding my baby girl. I felt the tingling behind my right eye, and knew a migraine was near. I felt a little perplexed. I was truly happy. I was holding my little blessing. I wasn't dealing with any stress.

I heard the words: *Please take my advice and write down what you are thinking about, as soon as you feel the migraine approaching.*

I placed my daughter in her bassinet.

I grabbed a piece of paper off the printer.

I found a pen in the kitchen drawer.

I sat down and attempted to replay my thoughts.

I was holding my baby.

"She is so beautiful. Look at all that hair. Oh, my precious baby. I will always protect you and keep you from harmful people. You will never be molested. You will never be raped. No family member or friends of the family will ever verbally assault my child. You are worthy of living a full life. You are worthy of love."

Paper and pen hit the floor, as I stumbled to the restroom to get my medicine. At the time I was on a medicine that came in a form of a strip which melted on your tongue.

I took my medicine and returned to the living room with baby girl. I sat down on the floor and sobbed years of held back tears. See, I had stopped myself from crying a couple of years ago. I was holding all power in my hands. I refused to cry because that meant I allowed someone to harm me, again.

No one was allowed to get too far into my heart. Tall, indestructible walls were built to keep out trespassers. When the hurtful memories were triggered, I would mentally exhaust myself in playing out scenarios on how and what I should have done. I practice what I would tell my persecutors. They made a once strong, smart girl into a victim. I created detail plans that ensured I would never hurt again. This plan only included what *I would do or say.*

I had convinced myself that I forgave everyone, but only a fool would forget and fail to prepare!

"And their sins and inequities will I remember no more."
— (Hebrews 10:17, KJV)

See there is a flaw in that thinking. It's a reason why people say, "Forgiveness is for you, not the other person. When you do not forgive that person, you allow them to continue to hurt you through the constant replay of the pain. It's like replaying a bad movie over and over. The scene never changes, no matter how many times you replay it. You can work out/ develop conversations to have with your persecutors, and may even be given the chance to tell them about the harm they inflicted upon you. The only problem is this practice does not guarantee immediate gratification or healing.

See my persecutors were either dead, or no longer a part of my life. Most times, the individuals move on and you are no longer in their thoughts.

Vengeance is not sweet and not yours to have. As long as you are seeking vengeance, you will never truly be happy and content.

> "Do not take revenge, my dear friends, but leave room for God's wrath, for it is written: "It is mine to avenge; I will repay," says the Lord."
>
> — (Romans 12:19, NIV)

The only answer is to seek God.

I was born and raised in church. I knew the Word of God, but I did not have a plan on how to implement God's Word during my tribulations.

I had to go back and revise my plan and begin with God.

Here's the plan I created to assist me in forgiving, for real. Not just in words, but in actions.

**Steps for Forgiving, for Real:**

1.  **Forgive yourself**- I truly had to stop blaming myself. I was not weak; I was a child. I was not stupid; I was with people who were supposed to love me. I did not give off the impression that I wanted to be abused. I had to truly stop saying, "I have a magnet that attracts bad things towards me." I declared I was worthy of happiness and God's glory. Philippians 4:9 (NIV) says, "Whatever you have learned or received or heard from me, or seen in me- put into practice. And the God of peace will be with you."

2.  **Take back power from the persecutors.** I declared they will no longer have permanent residence in my thoughts. Apostle Paul in Philippians 3:13 encouraged us to forget those things which are behind us. When the thoughts would resurface, I switched my focus. Initially I had to create happy places in my mind. I have an active mind, so I learned how to use it in a way that did not result in migraines. I cannot tell you how many times, in my mind, I was flying off on a private jet to some unknown paradise. As my relationship grows with God, I am able to focus on God's will through daily bible reading and prayer.

This takes time and continuous daily practice, so don't feel bad when you have to head to your private island, restaurant, shopping mall, or any other happy place in your mind.

3. **Truly forgive the persecutor(s) and place them in God's hands.** Romans 12:14 says, "Bless them which persecute you: bless, and curse not." I would pray: *Lord, I forgive them. I leave the hurt in your hands. Please keep me from seeking vengeance. Keep me from trying to reclaim the pain that I have placed in your hands. I know no weapon formed against me, shall prosper. You are an amazing, forgiving God. I will work diligently on being like your Son. In Jesus' Name. –Amen.*

"Love keeps no record of wrongs."- (1 Corinthians 13:5, NIV)

These three steps were implemented in heavy rotation in my daily routine. Sometimes I would allow my enemy to triumph over me, but God kept me. My daughter is now sixteen years old, and I have not had a migraine in fifteen years. All Glory to God!

My journey was and is not always traveled along rosy hills and beautiful waterfalls. The path becomes rough. Sometimes I'm truly crawling along a rocky path. I keep going and holding on to God. Through tears and blood, God favors me.

"Even though I walk through the valley of the shadow of death, I will fear no evil, for you are with me; your rod and your staff, they comfort me." –(Psalm 23:4, ESV)

You are worthy of God's love. He is right by your side. Seek Him, and you shall indeed find Him. He's waiting on you to follow his Word.

"Ask and it will be given to you; seek and you will find; knock and the door will be opened to you." – (Matthew 7: 7, NIV)

Forgive and Let Go. We were not created to guide our own steps.

Listen to God! Praise Him! Seek Him!

On the next page you will find some scriptures. Take some time and look up each scripture. Write down what God is speaking to you. If you don't have a bible, it's okay. Download Bible App on your phone or Google each scripture.

I do recommend you get a Bible. It's the one book everyone should have.

Before you read and meditate on God's Word, let me pray for you.

**My prayer for you and me:** *Lord, Jehovah Jireh! You are the Creator and Provider. You stay by our side, even when we fall astray. You are always there when we need you. For you never forsake us. Lord please use your Word and help us to forgive those who harm us. Use what the enemy meant for evil, and produce goodness, Lord. Use us as your witnesses to show your love and glory. Forgive us when we seek vengeance, while reminding us the vengeance is yours. Open your arms and keep us safe within your embrace. Give us the strength to be victors, not just survivors. As always, let your will be done in our lives. Thank you for past and future grace in our lives. In Jesus' name. Amen*

*Open your bible and read the following scriptures. Write down what God is saying to you:*

*Ephesians 1:7*

_____

_____

_____

_____

_____

_____

_____

*Daniel 9:9*

_____

_____

_____

_____

_____

_____

_____

_____

*Mathew 6: 9- 15*

_____

_____

_____

_____

_____

_____

_____

_____

*Psalms 32: 1- 9*

_____

_____

_____

_____

_____

_____

_____

_____


*Ephesians 4:32*

_____

_____

_____

_____

_____

_____

_____

_____

# CHAPTER TWO

# Man said, "No." God said, "Yes."

*"With man this is impossible, but with God all things are possible."*

*– (Mathew 19:26b, KJV)*

I didn't fully understand the unfairness of the world, or unfairness of man, until the age of eleven.

My parents officially split, and we had to move to the other side of the tracks. Literally!

Raising eight kids without any government support was not easy for my mother. She often worked two to three jobs and was going back to school at night to get her GED. Every other Saturday, we would head to Goodwill and sort through new arrivals for gently used clothes, shoes, books, and toys. Though we were struggling, my mother maintained high expectations for her kids.

She married at a young age and did not finish high school. She was dependent on a man to take care of her and their kids. Life taught her that she must be prepared to take care of herself, and education held the key to being independent.

All my mother children were required to maintain good grades. In order to get good grades, we had to maintain good behavior. We all knew that phone calls to my mother's job in reference to behavior, was not tolerated.

Everyone knew my mother expectations, including the school. We were to get good grades, so we can earn a scholarship to college.

So imagine what life was like when we moved to an area where nobody knew us or our mother. Add to the equation the district moving around school boundary zones, in effort to set all schools up for success.

On the first day at my new school in a new area of town, I found out quickly that you were judged by your location of housing.

The bus arrived in front of our apartment complex. Children, wearing first day of school clothes and shoes, eagerly boarded the bus. The bus arrived in front of the school, but the doors of the bus did not open.

We were told we had to wait on the principal to come to the bus, prior to unloading.

The bus sat in silence, as the children gazed out the window. We saw students being dropped off in fancy cars, wearing expensive shoes. Teachers hugging and welcoming students back to school.

I remember my stomach growling, as I wondered if breakfast would be as good as it was at my old school.

A man in a suit boarded the bus. He didn't seem happy, and I knew instantly he wasn't happy about us.

He looked down at us with disdain.

I don't know why, because I felt we looked similar to the other students. Everyone was clean. Boys showed off fresh haircuts. Girls wore new ribbons and bows in their hair.

He finally spoke, "You all will exit this bus quietly and walk in the line to the auditorium. You will be allowed to get breakfast after I set ground rules. Whatever you did at your old school, will not be allowed here."

As I walked in the line, I wondered if I would no longer be in orchestra. Did they not have an orchestra teacher? Would there be an honor roll celebration?

We sat in the auditorium for thirty minutes listening to "How things are done around here," and "Whatever foolishness you are used to doing, won't take place here."

We never did get breakfast.

The school did have orchestra. As an added plus, it was my same teacher. She moved among the middle schools during the day.

For career day, one of the teachers told the class that some of us were not smart enough for college, but still needed to pay attention to the presenters for there would be a quiz.

I wondered if she was referring to me.

There was an honor roll celebration, I just had to work extra hard to prove I was smart and understood what was being taught.

The sad thing was most teachers felt the way this teacher felt about us kids traveling in on the school bus. Their attitude affected how the other students viewed us.

Eventually it got better, once the teachers realized we were capable of learning what was being taught.

Words have a lingering hold on people. Hearing: "You are not smart enough. You live in the projects." "You won't be anything, but another statistic living off welfare."

Those were the nicer statements made towards me.

This school placed my self-worth at an all-time low.

Some educators tried to convince me I wouldn't go to college, because my mom doesn't have money. Family members said that even if I get a scholarship, I wouldn't graduate from college. I was even encouraged to look into trade school by a school counselor, when I had always been an honor roll student. The odds were stacked against me. When the majority of your family lived below the poverty line, there is a high possibility the next generation will live below poverty.

Even though I received a full scholarship to college, I always felt I was one step away from failing. Educators and family members had drastically affected my viewpoint on my abilities.

To be honest, I even anticipated the day of failure.

Though I worked hard in college, I spent most weekends in a club drinking my demons away. I relied on alcohol to clear my thoughts, so I could sleep at night. The only person waiting on me to get home was my Pitbull, Princess.

I share this part of my life to show you I did not always live according to the Word. In fact, I was so far gone; I felt God had turned away from me.

I was wrong, of course.

> "The Lord is my helper, and I will not fear what man shall do or say unto me."
> (Hebrews 13:6, KJV)

As graduation drew near, I interviewed before a committee for a teacher's aide position. I was working on my degree for teaching, and knew I wanted to work in a Title 1 school. I wanted children living in poverty to know that they could be anything they wanted to be, despite their current circumstances.

That dream was almost shattered. The moment I walked through the door, I felt like I was back in the middle school auditorium. In fact one of the men present looked very similar to that campus principal.

I haven't even spoken, but a sense of 'you are not worthy' washed over me.

I pushed past the nausea and answered each question with a smile.

At the end of the interview, the man, that looked like my middle school principal spoke. He suggested for me to switch career paths, for he didn't feel it was the best fit.

We all have had bad interviews, but this was a different experience, yet the same experience for me.

When I got to my car, I cried.

Once I pulled it together, I called my husband and shared what had occurred.

I then began to cry again.

I still remember exactly what my husband said to me on that day. I had let man win over me.

My husband's pep talk: "Why are you crying about what some buster told you? He interviewed you for fifteen minutes. Fifteen minutes does not qualify him as a decision-maker in your life. How many doctors told you that pregnancy was not for you and if you did get pregnant it would lead to a miscarriage? Those doctors did not have the final decision on your life, for I'm holding our baby girl as I fuss at you."

A month after graduation, I signed my first teaching contract!

When man says no, remember the servant of Elisha. When the Syrian Army went to Dothan to seize Elisha, his young servant was fearful and asked what they shall do. In 2 Kings, Elisha answered, "Fear not: for they that *be* with us are more than they that be with them." (2 Kings 6:16, KJV)

God's eyes are not closed. He sees all things and is working in favor for you. Don't allow man's words to keep you from walking towards what God has for you.

"No weapon that is formed against thee shall prosper, and every tongue that shall rise against thee in judgement thou shalt condemn. This is the heritage of the servants of the Lord, and the righteousness is of me, saith the Lord." – Isaiah 54:17 (KJV)

**Don't miss out on your blessing listening to *society*.**

**Steps to receiving the Yes, from God:**

1. **Check your situation.** Make sure you are aligned with God's purpose and will. God will not grant you a 'yes' to harm yourself or others. You need to be focused on God and He will grant your request. "For all the promises of God in Him are yes, and in Him Amen, to the glory of God through us." (2 Corinthians 1:20, NKJV) Make sure that you are living by the Word. James 1:22 warns us on deceiving our own selves.

2. **Believe your request will be granted in Jesus' name.** Know there is nothing too hard for God. He tells Abraham those exact words when Sarah thought it was funny for her to get pregnant at her age in Genesis 18:14. Just because it's impossible by man's standards, you have to remember God has the final say. It is not over. There is no period. In fact God shows-off in the impossible moments.

3. **Wait on God.** Everything is done in God's timing, not ours. Galatians 5:22 is a scripture that we should all remember: Patience is one of the fruit of spirits. Patience is truly not displayed until you are under trial and tribulations. Know that God has His reasons, even if we can determine the reason. "To everything there is a season, and a time to every purpose under the heaven." – (Ecclesiastes 3:1, KJV)

**Rely on God for the first and final answer.**

**My prayer for you and me:** *Lord, Jehovah. You are a mighty God. Your Word has been proven true myriads of times in the bible and within our lives. You open closed doors. Please heal our bodies and minds. Open doors that have been closed, yet keep doors closed that will bring harm. Hear your child's request. Let your will be done in our lives. With you God, all things are possible. Through your son, Jesus. Amen.*

Sometimes when we are waiting, we forget all the things God has already done. Our faith began to waiver. This is normal, but you have snap out of it. Thank God for what he has done, and then thank him in advance for what He is bringing in the future.

Before reading and mediating on this chapter' scriptures turn to the note pages in the back of the book and start a list of what God has already done in your life. Be specific! Target blessings that man could not and cannot guarantee to you.

*Open your bible and read the following scriptures. Write down what God is saying to you:*

*Leviticus6 20:24*

_____

_____

_____

_____

_____

_____

_____

_____

*Job 42: 10-17*

_____

_____

_____

_____

_____

_____

_____

_____

*1Peter 5:10*

_____

_____

_____

_____

_____

_____

_____

_____

_____

*Isaiah 41:10*

_____

_____

_____

_____

_____

_____

_____

*Philippians 4:6*

_____

_____

_____

_____

_____

_____

_____

*Psalm 34:17*

_____

_____

_____

_____

_____

_____

_____

_____

# CHAPTER THREE
# Finding Purpose

"Eye hath not seen, nor ear heard, neither have entered into the heart of man, the things which God hath prepared for them that love him."
— (I Corinthians 2:9, KJV)

*What exactly am I here for?*

*Lord, take this pain away.*

I was sitting on the restroom floor of my two- bedroom condo. It was the end of my sophomore year in college.

As I replayed the last ten to twelve years of my life, I could only recall bad memories.

The funny thing is, I wasn't sad. I was just tired of being mad.

I could hear my pitbull, Princess pacing in the kitchen. I had created a barricade, trash cans and chairs blocked the exit out of the kitchen to keep her in the kitchen.

I ran a hot bubble bath. As I sat down in the water, I pondered on how easy it would be to drown in the water.

The water began to cool, and my courage increased to finally slip below the water.

I heard a loud thunderous crash in my house.

Before I could even register what had occurred, I had an eighty pound Pitbull in the bath with me.

I love animals, but not to the point of sharing a bath. I jumped out and allowed her to enjoy what was left of the bubbles, for most of the water was on the floor.

As I cleaned up the restroom, I thought of a new plan for the next day. I was intent on ending my life for I could no longer continue to live with hurtful memories.

> "Don't be afraid, for I am with you. Don't be discouraged, for I am your God. I will strengthen you and help you. I will hold you up with my victorious right hand."
>
> - (Isaiah 41:10, NLT)

The next day, I locked Princess in her kennel. I knew my friend would be by later, and she would be free to live a happy life.

I went into the restroom, and opened a bottle of Tylenol.

As I emptied the pills in my mouth, I felt the wind leave me. My friend, Tina had arrived earlier than expected. She literally knocked the pills out of my mouth, and the bottle from my hand.

She held me in a tight hug. I don't remember her exact words, but I remember her convincing me I had a purpose to live and there was no pain worth taking my life.

I never did get a chance to thank Tina. I know God placed her in my life for this very moment.

Can I tell you that God had his hands on me? He wouldn't let me go. I had let Him go.

> "When tempted, no one should say, "God is tempting me." For God cannot be tempted by evil, nor does he tempt anyone; ¹⁴but each person is tempted when they are dragged away by their own evil desire and enticed."
>
> – (James 1:14, NIV)

For so long, I thought God was no longer with me. If He was with me, He was testing me, and I was failing.

At this time, I was no longer speaking to anyone in my family. I had convinced myself that if I disconnected from them, the painful memories would disappear.

My boyfriend, at the time, couldn't handle my self-destructive ways. He became more frustrated over time when he couldn't make me happy.

Here's the thing, nobody can make anyone do anything they don't want to do. I was busy solving my own problems without biblical principles. I had no time for happiness.

See when you are drowning in sorrow, it's extremely hard to see God's purpose in your life.

The day of the incident with Tina, I decided it was time to go home. Even though I was not speaking to anyone, my mother would send me letters. She would also tell me she loved me and that God was my helper. She would always end the letter with a scripture and reminder to pray to God. The next day, I drove back home for a two month summer stay.

Being one of eight kids truly was a blessing. I am the third to oldest, but they will all tell you that I'm the oldest. My siblings were happy to see me. They wanted to hear all about college. I could tell they really missed me and looked up to me. I was doing what nobody had done on my mother's side of the family. I was in college. Only one person on my father's side of the family had been to college.

I had to truly take some time and revel in the magnitude of having a praying mother. She knew God had a purpose for each of her children. I know for a fact that her deposited favor with God is why I was still alive.

As I laughed with my siblings over shared memories, I realized my life wasn't all bad. I remembered when I first start experiencing migraines in middle school; my dad would pick me up early and allow me to sleep. Afterwards we would get ice-cream from Baskin Robbins. Two scoops of buttered pecan on a waffle cone, please. I remember scaling the walls of the apartment building with my siblings to get to the park, when we knew we were under punishment. I have no idea how those bedsheets prevented us from breaking our necks.

My siblings shared some of the same heartbreaks with me. I was there to show them we were more than victims. We could pursue a higher education. We could be whatever we wanted to be, including business owners. Our past did not determine our future. My testimony was meant to demonstrate God's grace and mercy for others during difficult times.

The Marvin Sapp song, Grace and Mercy, reminded me of God's love and how Jesus' blood redeems me. See, before you can identify your purpose, you must know God's grace and mercy will get you through anything. Hebrews 13:6 lets you know God is your helper and man has no power over of you.

***True purpose is found when you live by God's Word and have faith in things not yet seen.***

**Steps for identifying your purpose in life:**

1.  **Read the bible.** A relationship with God has to be your primary focus. Life throws curve balls, and you need God to get through life. Psalms 119: 10-14 express the importance of praising and following God's Word.

2.  **Mediate on the Word.** Job 1:8 states we should mediate day and night. When you are preparing for an important test, you take time studying the material. You look over the information many times. You may even stay awake all night thinking about the test.

We should be the same with God. After reading the bible, take the time and mediate on what the Word is telling you. I found that starting my mornings with God and coffee ensures I am strong for any roadblock!

3. **Share the Word and your testimonies with others.** "Declare His glory among the nations. His wonders among all people." (Psalms 96:3, NKJV) It is our job to share God's glory with others. There are many people in need of a relationship with God, but may feel unworthy. Allow God to use you to reach them.

4. **Listen to God when he reveals your purpose.** Sometimes we respond like Jonah and take the long, unnecessary route, just to come back and do God's will. "Trust in the Lord with all your heart and lean not on your own understanding. In all your ways submit to him, and he will make your paths straight." (Proverbs 3:5-6, NIV) Know that all things work for the good of those that love God. – (Romans 8:28)

**Allow God to guide your footsteps.**

**My prayer for you and me:** Oh Heavenly Father. You are the God of all knowledge. You know each of us by name. You are the Lord who is, who was, and who is to come. Just as you take care of the birds and grass, you will surely take care of us. Change your servant, Lord, to what you have destined your servant to be. Cleanse our thoughts. Let your will be done in lives. We will listen and follow you. If we fall off the path, Lord, place us back on track. Give us the strength to keep going when times get tough. Through Christ Jesus we are redeemed. Amen.

Do not trust your own understanding. Remember, God's purpose for you is aligned to bible principles. Stay on the route of righteousness!

*Open your bible and read the following scriptures. Write down what God is saying to you:*

*Hebrews 11: 1*

_____

_____

_____

_____

_____

_____

_____

_____

*1 Timothy 6:17*

_____

_____

_____

_____

_____

_____

_____

_____

*Psalms 57:2*

_____

_____

_____

_____

_____

_____

_____

_____

*Mathew 6:33*

_____

_____

_____

_____

_____

_____

_____

*Philippians 4:11-12*

_____

_____

_____

_____

_____

_____

_____

_____

# CHAPTER FOUR
# Overcoming Untruths

"Cast your cares on the Lord and he will sustain you; he will never let the righteous be shaken. [23] But you, God, will bring down the wicked into the pit of decay; the bloodthirsty and deceitful will not live out half their days. But as for me, I trust in you."

(Psalm 55:22-23, NIV)

There's an old saying, "Hurt people, hurt people." This statement is very true, but not always understandable when you are going through the hurtful moment.

My parents' separation resulted in a move that placed us closer to my mother's side of the family. As with most families, there was unwarranted bitterness in the hearts of certain family members. The untruths they painted of my mother's children were often times unbearable. There were days that we were intentionally not fed. My mother would drop us off, while she juggled her two to three jobs, at a family member home to be taken care of in her absence. We were told my mother didn't leave food, even though we saw her bring in the food. Sometimes, we had to watch others eat the food that was meant for us. As the caretaker of my siblings, even though an adult was present, I tried to shield my siblings from the bitterness. I never told her about those horrific days, for I did not want to add an additional burden to her shoulders.

The daily reports usually consisted of many untruths about me: She's so disrespectful. She stole this... She did that...

On the way home or at home, my mother would reinforce behavior expectations in her absence. I think it eventually became too much for my mother, because she start allowing us to stay home when she went to work.

I was finally free of the untruths! Children make many mistakes on their own. No child needs any false mistakes added to the list.

When I became an adult, I separated myself from people in my family that struggled with honesty. Even little lies were unbearable for me to handle. I felt like I was always defending my character, and searching for motives behind the untruths told.

"He that worketh deceit shall not dwell within my house: he that telleth lies shall not tarry in my sight."- (Psalm 101:7, KJV)

This all hit the head of destruction, my fifth year of marriage. My marriage almost ended behind untruths.

People that I tried to build a relationship with for the sake of my husband, felt I was unworthy of my husband and my children. They would smile in my face, visit my home, and then meet among themselves and change conversations to reflect me in the negative light. Some of the individuals even made up fake arguments to share with others. Of course, when it came to light, each person involved attempted to wash their hands clean by sharing what the other person said.

My husband tried to keep the peace. His solution was to kick everyone out of our lives, and home. My childhood memories flooded my thoughts, and I became filled with anger. I wanted everyone to be brought to the floor, and their untruths and vindictive ways to be displayed. There were too many private conversations, and each person tried to tell me what the other person said and how they defended me. I wanted my husband to stand up for me and call each person out, but he didn't.

I felt hurt that he did not stand up for me, and filed for a divorce. I refused to be with someone that would not stand up for what was right and protect me. I knew my childhood played a role in my feelings. I know my mother knew some of what was being said was untrue, but she wanted to keep the peace with her family. She truly believed in forgiving and moving on. At one time I thought this was a weakness, now I understand the strength behind this ability. As I cried to my mother, she reminded me the battle was not mine to fight.

"What shall we then say to these things? If God be for us, who can be against us. Nay, in all these things we are more than conquerors through Him that loved us." – (Romans 8: 31, 38, KJV)

Fighting this battle could possibly tear apart all that God had given to me, and what was yet to come.

Once I calmed down, I realized God blessed me with my family. I realized it will take a family effort to ensure jealousy and bitterness does not enter our home or marriage. I also realized my husband loved me and only wanted me to be happy, even if that meant cutting his family from our lives. As I would never require my husband to do that, we came to happy median. As I shared earlier, marriage counseling helped me get through personal issues that I was carrying into my marriage.

My husband truly believed time would heal all pain, and some people needed time to themselves. I was totally confident in this belief, but I still needed to lean on my husband's strength. We sat down and discussed which individuals to have a discussion with, and which individuals will not play a role in our marriage or lives.

Be reminded Satan is busy roaming the earth and setting his eyes among God's servants. He maximizes on our weakness. I despised liars and had a true issue forgiving liars.

Those with untruths had no place in my heart or world. However, this is not my world and I have no control of people within this world.

The book of Job shows Satan's devises. Through it all Job, did not sin against God. Job 1:22 says, "In all this Job sinned not, nor charged God foolishly" (KJV). God is not a god of lies or heartaches. There is not a reason to charge God. Instead Job humbled and submitted himself to God. In return, Job was restored and blessed with more than he ever had. Job 42:17 says, "Job died being old and <u>full</u> of days."

What a great example Jesus provided when he was dealing with untruths. Be reminded Jesus was betrayed by one of his trusted disciples, Judas. He knew the day was coming and even foretold it to disciples. He was hurt, but he did not act out of anger.

Mathew 26:63 lets us know that Jesus held his peace, when a false witness was brought against him.

During the trail before Pilate, Jesus said nothing.

> On Cavalry, during his crucifixion, Jesus said, "Lord forgive them, for they know not what they do."
> — (Luke 23:34a, KJV)

We have to learn how to deal with others. All humans, including ourselves, are imperfect. Untruths will be spoken about you and against you. In Luke 17, Jesus tells us how to deal others. The first verse in this chapter says, "It is impossible but that offenses will come: but woe unto him, through whom they come" (KJV). Basically, we will deal with offenses. It is impossible to live a life free of offenses. People will cause us harm, and untruths will be spoken. Everybody carry their own emotional backpacks.

We have to forgive whether an apology occurs or not. Refer to chapter one of this book for the importance of forgiveness. You cannot allow untruths to determine how you live your life. Don't allow untruths to shake you and begin seeking vengeance or spend time on trying to prove the untruths are false.

When you are living a life with a clear conscience, you do not have to answer to anyone. Revelations 22:14 says, "Blessed are they that do his commandments, that they may have the right to the tree of life, and may enter in through the gates into the city" (KJV). Telling the truth and forgiving others is a part of God's commandments.

**Take heed and follow Jesus' footsteps.**

**Steps to overcoming untruths:**

1. **Determine the depth of the untruth**. Is this untruth based on a misconception or misunderstanding? If so, seek for understanding and clear up the misunderstanding. Take ownership of your part and apologize. Is this untruth based on a character assassination? Merriam-Webster defines character assassination as the slandering of a person usually with the intention of destroying public confidence in that person. This may involve exaggeration, misleading half-truths, or manipulations of facts to present an untrue picture you. If this is the case, proceed to step two.

2. **Discuss this untruth with the person.** Mathew 18:15-17 outlined the steps for completing this task. Luke 17:3 says, "Take heed to yourselves: If thy brother trespass against thee, rebuke him; and if he repents, forgive him." (KJV)

3. **Ask God to forgive them, and to help you to forgive and let go.** We will need God's forgiveness far more times than we will have to forgive individuals in our lives. Refer back to the scriptures in chapter one for additional support.

4. **Determine the continual impact of this person in your life**. Is this a person to love from afar? The key is to allow God to have his way in your life and theirs. Be the better person. When you are in their presence, follow Jesus' example.

5. **Know that people with speak untruths, regardless of how you are living your life.** Jesus lived a perfect life, yet he was physically torn apart and hung on a cross based on other's untruths about him.

**Do not return evil for evil. Allow God to use you as a vessel to share his love.**

**My prayer for you and I:** *Oh, Lord, thank you for sending your only begotten son, so I may be forgiven. In return, I will forgive seven times over. Let the words from your servant's mouth be true and acceptable in your sight. Use your word to strengthen your servant. Before coming to you, assist in guiding our footsteps to righting things with our brothers. Help your servant identify those to keep near and those to keep far. Take charge of our thoughts, Lord. For the battle is not ours, but yours. Please forgive those who sin against your servant. Use your servant to draw others into a relationship with you. All these things, in Jesus' name. Amen.*

*Open your bible and read the following scriptures. Write down what God is saying to you:*

*Mathew 12: 36- 37*

_____

_____

_____

_____

_____

_____

_____

_____

*Romans 12:4-8*

_____

_____

_____

_____

_____

_____

_____

_____

*James 4: 11-12*

_____

_____

_____

_____

_____

_____

_____

_____

*1 John 4:4*

_____

_____

_____

_____

_____

_____

_____

*1 Peter 3: 8- 17*

_____

_____

_____

_____

_____

_____

_____

# CHAPTER FIVE
## Victor vs. Survivor!

"I can do all things through Christ which strengthen me."
– (Philippians 4:13, KJV)

Having a daughter really put a different perspective on life. I moved from being a survivor to a victor.

The bible wasn't written just to retell stories of God's glory, but it was written for our sake. In Romans chapter 4, Apostle Paul let us know the bible was written for us, believers of Christ. We have to have faith that God has the final say and He will deliver us from the pain.

God thought I was worthy of saving, and Jesus Christ thought I was worth dying for. He never wanted me to just be a survivor, but a victor.

Survival is the first step. Merriam-Webster defines survive as to remain alive or in existence. After years of molestation, I was still alive.

I was raped, but alive.

Broken and abused, but alive.

Still alive to tell the story, but not thriving.

I abused alcohol to get through tough days, where pain stood in front of every action and thought.

My undiagnosed OCD allowed me to have temporary relief of pain. My strong desire for order allowed me to succeed in school, but college presented its own challenges. Monday through Thursday, I was engrossed in school work and studying. As an athletic trainer, I would travel with the football and track team. The weekends provided too much idle time. When I would lose control of my thoughts, I would use alcohol to clear my thoughts.

I remember the time I was sitting on my back porch with Princess. Upon hearing a door close in the front of the duplex, she took off towards the front of our home. By the time I got there, Princess was playing a game of chase with the neighbor.

I called her name, and she came to me.

Of course the neighbor was mad, and was screaming profanity. I remember her yelling, "Train your dog and lay off the bleach." See I used cleaning to maintain control. I had the cleanest base boards and floor. My duplex was sterilized daily.

She moved out and the landlord had a talk with me. She thanked me for keeping the duplex spotless, but asked me to be more flexible with the neighbors. I never understood what that quite meant until I was older. At the time, I just thought I had to do a better job in hiding my illness. I continue to clean, and continue to drink.

Contrary to popular beliefs, when you are underage, it is difficult to buy alcohol. You could get others to purchase it for you, but then others would realize you have a habit. I found going to clubs the easy way to get my fix. I would allow others to buy me drinks, until I became numb. Then I would get in my car and drive an hour back to campus.

I would then spend the next day sterilizing everything, until night fell. This cycle would repeat itself each weekend.

Alcohol and drug abuse is only a temporary fix. It cannot get rid of pain inflicted upon your body and mind by another human. This behavior usually leads to the abuse of the substance of choice.

I was a survivor of tragic events, but it was not enough.

"The Lord is my rock, and my fortress, and my deliverer; my God, my strength, in whom I will trust; my buckler, and the horn of my salvation, and my high tower."- (Psalm 18:2, KJV)

Between the ages of two through seven, my daughter was a force to be reckoned with. She did not change herself to fit the norms around her. She refused to take any punishment which she felt she did not earn. I would plead with her each morning to listen to her daycare or school teacher, even if she felt they were being unfair. She even brought home a list of unfair things her teacher did during the school day to defend how she ended with a sad face on her folder.

There was this one particular day that really hit a chord. She was in the first grade, and her classroom was right next to my classroom. Her teacher entered my classroom, asking me to do something about my child. Here I was the teacher that received behavior kids, and developed scholars, yet my child was struggling.

I had took all her toys at home, and had many conversations. She even was spanked. The behavior did not change and she seemed to truly be content within any and all punishments.

Her teacher confirmed she had changed her seat in the classroom and removed station privileges, yet my child was still refusing to work.

I asked the teacher to cover my class, as I took my daughter to the car.

When we got to the car, I didn't know what to do or say. I asked, "What can I do to help you get your work completed?"

She lifted her head and said, "Nothing. I'm not doing the work over again. I made a 100, and because everyone else failed all the papers went to the trash can. She passed out new copies, and told the class that we will do it again. I am not doing it again. I know you are sad, and I will be punished when I get home."

I was at a true loss.

Still trying to support the teacher and ensure I have all the information, I asked, "What did you say when she put your paper in the trash?"

She smiled at me and said, "I told her as long as you wrote my 100 in the gradebook! That's why I have no centers, unless I do it over again. So I said, I guess I won't ever have centers!"

I couldn't do anything but smile at my little fighter. At the age of seven, she taught me that nobody has control of your happiness. It doesn't matter what they say or do, or any consequence you have to endure, only you have control of your happiness.

She was willing to take the punishment at school and home to remain who she was as a happy first grader.

I was still living a survivors' life, not drinking, but not thriving. I stopped drinking pain away after I found out I was pregnant with my miracle baby. I wanted to ensure I was the best mother for her. I was just moving through the motions, again.

Whenever anybody would ask my husband how he was doing, he would reply, "I'm winning." I used to get irritated for I didn't truly understand what that meant.

A victor know they are winners/conquerors. They know God has not left their side. The enemies' goal is to defeat you, but you have to allow God to work a miracle for you.

In the book of Genesis we learn of Joseph. His jealous brothers sold him into slavery and convinced their father he was dead. Joseph didn't just survive the hurt, lies, and imprisonment.

He came out as a victor. Genesis 39:21 says, "But the Lord was with Joseph and showed him mercy, and gave him favor in the sight of the keeper in prison" (KJV).

When Joseph comforted his brothers in Genesis 50:20 he said, "But as for you, you meant evil against me, but God meant if for good in order to bring about his present result, to save many people alive." (NKJV)

What a great feeling of relief when you are able to identify the good. Move your sorrow out of the way, and look for what God wants to showcase within you to bring glory to His kingdom.

I choose to follow Paul's example. After being beaten and thrown into prison, Paul and Silas prayed and sang praises to God. They sung so loud the other prisoners heard the praise. Hearing their praise, God created a great earthquake. That night Paul brought many to God. Acts 16:33 says, "And he (jailer) took them the same hour of the night, and washed their stripes; and was baptized, he and all his, straightaway." (KJV)

Use your testimony and praises to draw others into God's Kingdom. Thank God for being in control of your life and allow him to make changes within you. You are here to defeat the enemy and become a victor, not survive the enemy.

**Steps to become a victor:**

1. **Live in the present.** Don't allow your thoughts to place you in a victim mentality. We were destined to live a happy life. Adam sinned brought death, but Jesus' death brought life. Live again. "Now the Lord of Peace himself give you peace always by all means. The Lord be with you all." (2 Thessalonians 3:16, KJV) Allow the Lord to give you peace. Worrying only creates unnecessary anxiety. God has you in His hands. – Mathew 6: 25-34

2. **Identify the good.** Make a difference in other's lives. Mathew 5:16 says, "Let your light so shine before men, that they may see your good works, and glorify your Father which is in heaven" (KJV). Jesus' grace allows us to finish the race. "Fight the good fight of the faith. Take hold of the eternal life to which you were called when you made your good confession in the presence of many witnesses." (1 Timothy 6:12, NIV) We are all apart of God's body. Let His will be done within our lives.

3. **Praise God.** It truly confuses the enemy and helps eliminate the negative thoughts and memories. 2 Chronicles 20:22 says, when discussing Jehoshaphat defeat over Judah's enemies, "And when they began to sing and to praise, the Lord set ambushments against the children of Ammon, Moab, and mount Seir, which were come against Judah; and they were smitten" (KJV). The enemy became so confuses they killed one another. Praise also help us shift focus from ourselves to God. You cannot wallow in your pain and praise God at the same time. Try singing this gospel verse or your favorite gospel

hymn without smiling: *Our God is an awesome God, He reigns from heaven above, with wisdom, power, and love. Our God is an awesome God. He reigns. Forever and Ever!*

It's impossible, because you are only thinking of God's greatness.

**My prayer for you and me:** *Lord, God, Come into our mind and hearts. Wash us clean of hurt and pain. Reveal the good of this tragic event. Use me, Lord. Let the words of my lips and the actions of my body be acceptable to you. We shall rejoice in you Lord all day and every night. Guide me in using your Word to bring others in the celebration of praising your name. Thank you for allowing your son to live and die to wash us free of our sin. Thank you in advance for what is yet to come. In Jesus' name. -Amen*

*Open your bible and read the following scriptures. Write down what God is saying to you:*

*Jeremiah 29:11*

_____

_____

_____

_____

_____

_____

_____

*Romans 8:28*

_____

_____

_____

_____

_____

_____

_____

*Mark 14:36*

_____

_____

_____

_____

_____

_____

_____

_____

*Psalm 84:11*

_____

_____

_____

_____

_____

_____

_____

_____

*Hebrews 12:2*

_____

_____

_____

_____

_____

_____

_____

_____

# Praise List

*Take a moment and make your praise list. Think of all the good God has done for you. Write down the big and small moments. As you create the list, thank God again for that blessing. If you need more space, utilize the extra note page in the back of the book.*

*Examples: "Thank you Lord for using your angels and keeping me from running into the back of that truck." "Thank you Lord for the five dollars, I found in my pockets this morning. I was able to get to work today." Refer back to this list when a crisis arises, and then thank God in advance for getting you through the crisis.*

1. _____

2. _____

3. _____

4. _____

5. _____

6. _____

7. _____

8. _____

9. _____

10. _____

11. _____

12. _____

13. _____

14. _____

# Victor's Playlist

1. *Hold on- Change is Coming by Sounds of Blackness*

2. *Order my Steps by Mighty Clouds of Joy*

3. *Change Me by Tamela Mann*

4. *My Testimony by Marvin Sapp*

5. *Praise on the Inside by J. Moss*

6. *I Trust You by James Fortune and Fiya*

7. *Worth by Anthony Brown and Group Therapy*

8. *The Battle is Not Yours by Yolanda Adams*

9. *Praise Him in Advance by Marvin Sapp*

10. *I Told the Storm by Greg O'Quin and Joyful Noyze*

11. *God Favored Me by Hezekiah Walker and Love Fellowship Crusaders*

12. *I Won't Complain by Rev. Paul Jones*

# References

*Scripture quotations marked (NIV) are taken from the Holy Bible, New International Version®, NIV®. Copyright © 1973, 1978, 1984, 2011 by Biblica, Inc.™ Used by permission of Zondervan. All rights reserved worldwide. www.zondervan.com The "NIV" and "New International Version" are trademarks registered in the United States Patent and Trademark Office by Biblica, Inc.™*

*Scripture quotations from The Authorized (KJV) Version. Rights in the Authorized Version in the United Kingdom are vested in the Crown. Reproduced by permission of the Crown's patentee, Cambridge University Press*

*Scripture quotations marked (NLT) are taken from the Holy Bible, New Living Translation, copyright ©1996, 2004, 2015 by Tyndale House Foundation. Used by permission of Tyndale House Publishers, Inc., Carol Stream, Illinois 60188. All rights reserved.* Scripture quotations are from the ESV® Bible (The Holy Bible, English Standard Version®), copyright © 2001 by Crossway, a publishing ministry of Good News Publishers. Used by permission. All rights reserved.

*Merriam- Webster dictionary, s.v. "survive," accessed May 24, 2019, https://merriam-webster.com/dictionary/survive*

*Merriam- Webster dictionary, s.v. "character assassination," accessed May 24, 2019, https://www.merriam-webster.com/dictionary/character%20assassination?src=search-dict-box*

## *Local Church*

Find a local your church:

[www.church.org](www.church.org)

Visit the church for at least a month to determine if this is the right fit for you. Ensure the church is a bible-based church, which means, the sermon is centered on scriptures read as written in the bible.

# Extra Note Page

# Special Thanks

*I must first thank God for using me as a vessel to share His Word. He has kept me and provide strength when I was nothing. I am still nothing, without Him.*

*I must thank my mother for always praying for me. Through her covenant with God, I have His mercy.*

*I cannot thank Tina enough for allowing God to use her to intervene in my life.*

*I truly thank my husband, Carl, for demonstrating patience and understanding. He truly balance me.*

*Special thanks to my two children, Allison and Caden. Because of you two, I'm a better person.*

*Special thanks and love to Wendy and Ken. God used these wonderful people to keep me on track of completing this book to share God's glory.*

*Wendy's keen eye in editing ensure I finished this project. She provided a listening ear, with sound advice.*

*God truly places individuals in your life to ensure His will is done.*

**How is God using you?**

Printed in the United States
By Bookmasters